Greetings

Building Vocabulary

A. Choose and fill in the blanks to make sentences.

country	science	friend	people
volleyball	famous	shake hands	geography

1.

This is my _____friend_____, Jessica.
She is my classmate.

2.

Portugal is a smaller _____
than Spain.

3.

_____ are watching
the soccer game.

4.

Koreans often _____
with bowing.

5.

The _____ movie star
wrote her autobiography.

6.

_____ is the study of the earth's
landscapes, places and environments.

7.

I play both tennis and _____.

8.

We learn _____, history, and
geography at school.

3

B. Match the jobs, pictures and what the workers do.

1. porter ● ● a. ● ● paint something as a job

2. painter ● ● b. ● ● serve food in a restaurant

3. waitress ● ● c. ● ● make pictures using a camera

4. singer ● ● d. ● ● sing on a stage

5. photographer ● ● e. ● ● carry things for people at a hotel

C. Circle the correct words and complete the sentences.

1.

Kevin and Lisa are _____.
(teachers / students)

2.

It's nice _____ you, David.
(to meet / meeting)

3.

Are Suji and Jennifer in the same science
_____?
(classroom / class)

4.

_____ are you from?
(What / Where)

4

First Step in

English Discussion

1

Workbook

I am books

Contents

A. Look at the text. Read it and complete the table. Then add your own information.

Hi! My name's Olivia. I'm eleven years old and I'm a student. I'm from Italy. My best friend is Maria. She's Italian, too. We're classmates. My favorite school subjects are English and history. My favorite star is Britney Spears. She's great! What about you? Please write soon.

Name: Olivia

Age: **1.** _____eleven years old_____

From: **2.** _____

Favorite school subjects: **3.** _____

Favorite star: **4.** _____

Name(You): **5.** _____

Age: **6.** _____

From: **7.** _____

Favorite school subjects: **8.** _____

Favorite star: **9.** _____

B. Match the sentences to the responses.

1. Are you from Egypt? _____c_____ •   • a. No, I don't.

2. Where are you from? _____ •   • b. They're from Canada.

3. Hi, my name's Suji Kim. _____ •   • c. Yes, I am.

4. Do you live in Mexico City? _____ •   • d. No, she isn't. She's from Australia.

5. Where are your friends from? _____ •   • e. Hi, my name's Peter.

6. Is your teacher from the U.S.? _____ •   • f. We're from Singapore.

Super Writing 1

A. Circle the correct words and rewrite the sentences.

1.

My name is Sarah Lee. Everyone has a (smartphone / name).

⇨ _____

2.

Are you (with / from) the United States? – Yes, I am.

⇨ _____

3.

Who is your favorite (teacher / sport)?

⇨ _____

4.

I (live / alive) in Seoul. I'm eleven years old.

⇨ _____

B. Write the sentences as in the example.

1. My favorite subject is history. _I'm good at English, too._ _____

(English)

2. My favorite subject is English. _____

(gymnastics)

3. My favorite subject is music. _____

(geography)

4. My favorite subject is science. _____

(biology)

● 1~3 Unscramble the words to make sentences.
● 4~6 Sentence Transformation. / N(Negative), Q(Question)

1.

| have | our pets | . | names |

⇨ _____

2.

| people | greeting | . | bow | in | , | in some Asian cultures |

⇨ _____

3.

| a hug and a kiss | each other | . | with | greet | people |

⇨ _____

4.

They may shake hands. (N)

⇨ _____

5.

Steve is from Italy. (Q)

⇨ _____

6.

She's in the school volleyball team. (Q)

⇨ _____

Super Speaking!

A. Listen to the dialog again. Please circle the correct words. ⊙ Track 5

A: Hello. My name is Steven Carson. What's your name?

B: Hi. My name is Jennifer Miller, but (a) called / (b) call me Jen.

A: It's nice to (a) meet / (b) met you, Jen.

B: Nice to meet you, too.

A: Where are you from, Jen?

B: I'm from Italy. (a) Where / (b) What about you?

A: I'm from Mexico.

B: I'm sorry. What's your last name again? Cason?

A: Actually, it's Carson.

B: How do you spell that?

A: C-A-R-S-O-N

B: What's your favorite (a) subject / (b) object ?

A: My favorite subject (a) are / (b) is geography. What's your favorite sport?

B: Volleyball. I'm in the school volleyball team.

A: Oh, good. Suji is here.

B: Who's Suji?

A: She's my classmate. We're in the same science class.

B: Where's she from?

A: She's from Korea. (a) Let's / (b) It's go and say hello.

B. Let's Talk Ask and answer the questions about the dialog with your partner.

1. Where is Jennifer from?

⇨ She is from _____.

2. What is Steven's favorite subject?

⇨ _____ is geography.

3. Is Jennifer in the school soccer team?

⇨ No, _____ . She is _____.

4. Are Suji and Jennifer classmates?

⇨ No, _____ . _____ are classmates.

Language Focus! S + Be / S + Be + Not / Be + S ...?

Grammar Focus 1

● **Affirmatives / Negative of Be**

She is Tiffany.	He is Peter.
They are teachers.	They aren't doctors.
They are old.	They aren't young.

Positives			Negatives			
Pronouns	Be	Contractions	Pronouns	Be	Not	contractions
I	am	I'm	I	am		I'm not
You	are	You're	You	are		You aren't
He/She/It	is	He's/She's/It's	He/She/It	is	not	He/She/It isn't
We/They	are	We're/They're	We/They	are		We/They aren't

Grammar Focus 2

● **The Verb Be : Yes/No questions**

Q: Is he a pianist?
A: No, he isn't. He is a pilot.

Q: Are they nurses?
A: Yes, they are.

Questions	Answers	
Am I ~?	Yes, you are.	No, you aren't.
Are you ~?	Yes, I am.	No, I'm not.
Is he / she / it ~?	Yes, he/she/it is.	No, he/she/it isn't.
Are we ~?	Yes, you are.	No, you aren't.
Are you ~?	Yes, we are.	No, we aren't.
Are they ~?	Yes, they are.	No, they aren't.

A. Look at the pictures and complete the sentences.

1.

It ___is not___ a lion.
It ___is___ a tiger.

2.

We _____ teachers.
We _____ doctors.

3.

He _____ a tennis player.
He _____ a soccer player.

4.

I _____ happy.
I _____ sad.

5.

They _____ oranges.
They _____ apples.

6.

She _____ a lawyer.
She _____ an architect.

B. Complete the questions and answers.

1. _____Are_____ they Tom's friends?   Yes, _____they are_____ .

2. _____ she an English teacher?   No, _____ .

3. _____ you a student at this school?   Yes, _____ .

4. _____ it a new smart phone?   No, _____ .

Super Speaking

● Look at the example and practice with a partner. Use the cues given. Then change roles and practice again.

Gyuri / Korea
an actress / 28 years old

A: Where is _____Gyuri_____ from?
B: She is from _____Korea_____ .
A: What is her job?
B: She is _____an actress_____ .
A: How old is she?
B: She is _____28 years old_____ .

Will Smith / America
a movie star / 41 years old

Megan Fox / America
an actress / 25 years old

Jackie Chan / Hong Kong
an action movie star / 57 years old

Building Vocabulary

A. Choose and fill in the blanks to make sentences.

> family   straight black hair   grandmother   left-handed
>
> photographer   swimming   nurses   grandfather

1.

This is my ___grandfather___ .

2.

Kathy is _____ .

3.

There are four people in my
_____ .

4.

Sujin has _____ .

5.

My uncle is a _____ .

6.

They are _____ .

7.

I live with my grandfather and
_____ .

8.

I like sports and my favorite sport is
_____ .

B. Look at the picture of Peter and his family. How are the people related to Peter? Write the correct word next to each family member.

aunt	grandfather	older sister	grandparents	mother	uncle	father

1. My mother's sister is my _____aunt_____. Her name is _____Tiffany_____.

2. My mother's parents are my ___grandparnets___. Their names are _____.

3. My grandfather's son is my _____uncle_____. His name is _____.

4. My mother's father is my _____. His name is _____.

5. My parents' daughter is my _____. Her name is _____.

6. My mother's husband is my _____. His name is _____.

7. My father's wife is my _____. Her name is _____.

A. Read and complete David Beckham's family tree.

David Beckham is from London, England. His full name is David Robert Joseph Beckham. He is a very famous soccer player. His hair is blond and his eyes are blue. He was born on the 2nd of May 1975. His mother is Sandra and his father is Ted. His wife is Victoria Adams. Their two sons are Brooklyn and Romeo. Their two puppies are Snoop and Puffy.

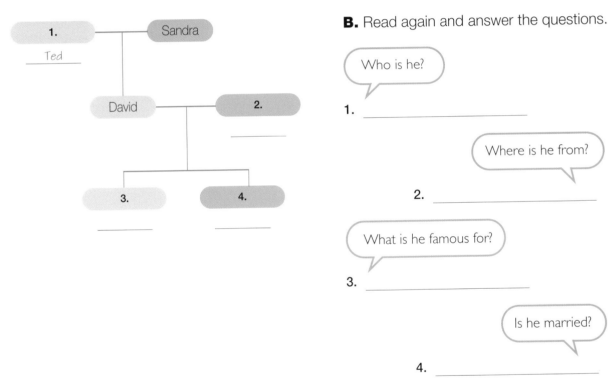

B. Read again and answer the questions.

Who is he?

1. _____

Where is he from?

2. _____

What is he famous for?

3. _____

Is he married?

4. _____

C. Match the questions and answers.

1. Do you have any brothers and sisters?　•

2. Does he have a sister?　•

3. Does she have any children?　•

4. Are these your cousins?　•

5. Do you have any children?　•

6. Do they have any brothers or sisters?　•

　• a. Yes, she does. She has a daughter.

　• b. Yes, we do. We have two boys.

　• c. Yes, I do. I have three sisters:
　　　Sunny, Grace, and Jane.

　• d. No, they don't.

　• e. No, he doesn't.

　• f. Yes, they're twins.

Super Writing 1

A. Circle the correct phrases or words and rewrite the sentences.

1.

   This is my family. These are (my / your) parents.

   ⇨ _____

2.

   Do you have (some / any) brothers or sisters?

   ⇨ _____

3.

   My mother has (straight black / curly brown) hair and has black eyes.

   ⇨ _____

B. Match the phrases and write the sentences as in the example.

On the weekend, my family often..

1. buys some books	at home
2. eats out	at a department store
3. watches DVDs	at a bookstore
4. goes shopping	at a family restaurant

1. On the weekend, my family often buys some books at a bookstore.

2. _____

3. _____

4. _____

● 1∼3 Unscramble the words to make sentences.
● 4∼6 Sentence Transformation. / N(Negative), Q(Question)

1.

left-handed | Scott | . | like his father | is

⇨ _____

2.

your mother | look | you | . | just like

⇨ _____

3.

have | . | you | both | a beautiful smile

⇨ _____

4.

Your brother looks like your grandfather. (N)

⇨ _____

5.

Your mother has blond straight hair. (Q)

⇨ _____

6.

You are close to your brother or sister. (Q)

⇨ _____

– Yes, _____.

Super Speaking!

A. Listen to the dialog again. Please circle the correct words or write the missing words. ⏺ Track 14

A: Is this your mother?

B: Yes, that's my mother.

A: Wow! You ⬚ (a) look / (b) looked ⬚ just like your mother. You ___b_____ have a beautiful smile.

B: We are also ⬚ (a) right-handed / (b) left-handed ⬚ .

Do you look like your mother or father?

A: I look like my father.

B: Oh, what does he do?

A: He is a ___s_____ and my mother is a homemaker.

B: Wow! And ⬚ (a) where / (b) what ⬚ about your brother?

A: He's a ___w_____ photographer.

B: What an ⬚ (a) interesting / (b) interest ⬚ family! What does your brother look like?

A: He has black straight hair and brown ___e_____ .

B. **Let's Talk** Read and repeat the dialog. Then use the speaking cards to practice it with your partner.

A: Do you look more like your father or mother?

B: I look more like my ❶ ___mother___ .

We both have ❷ ___brown eyes___ .

A: Wow! What does ❸ ___she___ do?

B: ❸ ___She___ is a ❹ ___nurse___ and

my ❺ ___father___ is a ❻ ___doctor___ .

❶ father
❷ black eyes
❸ he
❹ vet
❺ mother
❻ chef

❶ mother
❷ curly brown hair
❸ she
❹ architect
❺ father
❻ pilot

Grammar Focus 1

● **Possessive Adjectives**

- We use possessive adjectives before nouns to show that something belongs to someone.

She is reading her book.

That is my house.

These are the tennis rackets.
These are their rackets.

Singular		Plural	
Subject pronoun	Possessive adjective	Subject pronoun	Possessive adjective
I	my	we	our
you	your	you	your
he	his		
she	her	they	their
it	its		

Grammar Focus 2

● **Possessive Nouns**

- We use 's (apostrophe s) or ' (apostrophe) to talk about things that belong to people.

- We use an apostrophe(') + -s to a singular noun or an irregular plural noun. We use only an apostrophe(') to a plural noun ending in -s.

It is John's car.

I'm wearing my
roommate's shoes.

children's books	men's clothing
people's lives	teacher's office
John's bag	the girl's name
sharks' teeth	the cat's tail
the man's hat	runners' shoes

A. Make 's or s' possessive structures.

1. The dog belongs to Joe ⇨ _Joe's dog_

2. The house belongs to Ann ⇨ _____

3. The book belongs to Olivia ⇨ _____

4. The money belongs to the children ⇨ _____

5. The hat belongs to the man ⇨ _____

B. Look at the pictures and write as in the example.

1.

I have a handkerchief.
It's ___my handkerchief___ .

2.

She has a scarf.
It's _____ .

3.

They have a car.
It's _____ .

4.

We have hats.
They're _____ .

5.

He has a bicycle.
It's _____ .

Super Speaking

● Look at the example and practice with a partner. Use the cues given. Then change roles and practice again.

What is Peter's favorite hobby?

His favorite hobby is reading.

Peter / hobby / ?
⇨ reading

Nancy / food / ? ⇨ pizza

Steve / movie / ? ⇨ "Batman"

Abigail / sport / ? ⇨ soccer

Building Vocabulary

A. Choose and fill in the blanks to make sentences.

tourists	fantastic beaches	packing	island
go on a trip	airplane	sunbathing	scuba diving

1.

We're _____ our suitcase now.

2.

I'm going to _____ around Europe.

3.

Travelling by _____ is very convenience.

4.

The beautiful island of Phuket is famous for its _____.

5.

London's city center is crowded with _____.

6.

She's _____ on the beach.

7.

The man is _____.

8.

Have you ever been to Jeju _____?

B. Read the definitions and complete the words.

1. to rest and allow yourself to become calm

| r | | | | |

2. to pay money regularly to use a house, room, office, etc. that belongs to someone else

| | e | | |

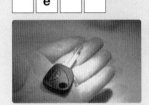

3. to make reservations for something in advance

| | | o | k |

4. the holiday or vacation spent together by a newly married couple

| h | o | n | e | y | | | |

C. Look and check the correct words.

1.

restroom _____
restaurant _____

2.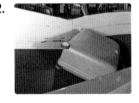

brochure _____
baggage _____

3.

bridge _____
building _____

4.

scary _____
funny _____

A. Let's Talk Look at the box below. What did you do last summer? Ask and answer questions as in the example.

> e.g. A: Did you travel abroad? B: Yes, I did.
>   A: Did you stay at a hotel? B: No, I didn't.

travel abroad? (✓)	sunbathe in the mornings? ( )
stay at a hotel? (✗)	collect any shells? ( )
swim every day? ( )	watch the sun set? ( )
go fishing? ( )	see yachts and colorful corals? ( )
meet any new people? ( )	ride a banana boat? ( )

B. Imagine that you went abroad last year and write about your holiday. Begin like this:

Last summer I traveled abroad. I went to ...

C. Complete the dialog with the sentences *a-d*.

a. Because I'm going on a trip tomorrow.

b. When are you leaving?

c. Are you coming to Olivia's party tonight?

d. At five o'clock.

Kevin: Hello, Lisa. ❶ _____ c _____

Lisa: No, I'm not.

Kevin: Why not?

Lisa: ❷ _____

Kevin: Really? Where to?

Lisa: We're going to Spain. My grandparents live there.

Kevin: That's great. ❸ _____

Lisa: Tomorrow morning. ❹ _____

21

Super Writing 1

A. Circle the correct words and rewrite the sentences.

1.

My hotel is very nice and (comfortable / dirty).

⇨ _____

2.

(Korea / Seoul) is a big city with a lot of new buildings.

⇨ _____

3.

Did you meet (some / any) new people there?

⇨ _____

4.

Its (population / popular) is about 200 million and the official language is Portuguese.

⇨ _____

B. Look at the pictures. Write the city names and complete the sentences as in the example.

Cities
New York
Paris
Rome
London

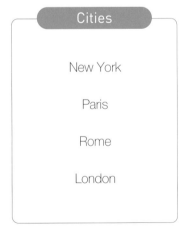

1. City [_____]

the Colosseum the Pantheon

2. City [_____]

London Bridge Big Ben

3. City [_____]

the Eiffel Tower   the Louvre Museum

4. City [_____]

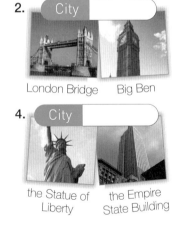

the Statue of Liberty   the Empire State Building

1. If _you go to Rome_ , you will see the Colosseum and _the Pantheon_ .

2. If _____ , _____ and _____ .

3. If _____ , _____ and _____ .

4. If _____ , _____ and _____ .

Super Writing 2

● 1~3 Unscramble the words to make sentences.
● 4~7 Sentence Transformation. / N(Negative), Q(Question)

1.
| in the world | . | one of | is | the longest rivers | the Amazon |

⇨ _____

2.
| Patong beach | the most popular beach | . | among tourists | is |

⇨ _____

3.
| delicious and cheap | . | the food | is |

⇨ _____

4.
You have been to Korea. (Q)

⇨ _____

5.
We're going to go to Switzerland in December. (N)

⇨ _____

6.
They're going to travel by train. (Q)

⇨ _____

7.
We're going to arrive in Seoul on Saturday afternoon. (N)

⇨ _____

Super Speaking!

A. Listen to the dialog again. Please circle the correct words. Track 21

A: Hi. How can I | (a) helped / (b) help | you?

B: I'd like to book package tour to Jeju island.

A: Yes, good choice. Jeju island is | (a) absolutely / (b) absolute | beautiful this time of year.

How many people do you want to book for?

B: Two – myself and my new wife. It's for our honeymoon.

A: Congratulations! You | (a) could / (b) couldn't | have picked a more romantic island.

When are you looking to go?

B: From July 21st until August 6th.

A: Would you like | (a) choosing / (b) to choose | a hotel from this brochure?

B: Okay. Ah, what about this one?

B. Let's Talk Look at the example and practice with a partner. Use the words below. Then change roles and practice again.

Steve / London / ?
⇨ three days

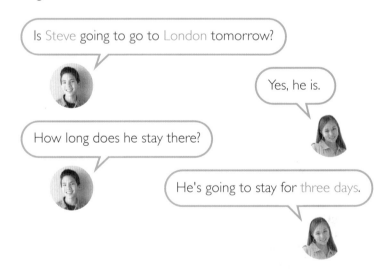

Is Steve going to go to London tomorrow?

Yes, he is.

How long does he stay there?

He's going to stay for three days.

Bill / Seoul / ?
⇨ two weeks

Ellen / Sydney / ?
⇨ five days

Eric and Sue / Phuket / ?
⇨ six days

Grammar Focus 1

● Future: be going to

She's going to **go to** Hong Kong tomorrow morning.

Alice is not going to drink juice. She's going to eat the apple.

Affirmative	
Subject + be	going to + base verb
I am	
You are	
We are	going to eat the apple.
They are	
She/He/It is	

Negative	
Subject + be	not going to + base verb
I am	
You are	
We are	not going to eat the apple.
They are	
She/He/It is	

Grammar Focus 2

● Yes/No Questions: be going to

Q: Are they going to watch a soccer game tonight?

A: No, they aren't. They're going to study in the library.

Questions (Be + Subject + going to ~?)		
Am I going to ~?	⇨	Yes, you are. / No, you aren't.
Are you going to ~?	⇨	Yes, I am. / No, I am not.
Are we going to ~?	⇨	Yes, you are. / No, you aren't.
Are they going to ~?	⇨	Yes, they are. / No, they aren't.
Is she going to ~?	⇨	Yes, she is. / No, she isn't.
Is he going to ~?	⇨	Yes, he is. / No, he isn't.
Is it going to ~?	⇨	Yes, it is. / No, it isn't.

A. Look at the chart and make sentences with *be going to*.

My Winter Vacation Plan			
1. learn to ski	√	2. go to the museum	X
3. go to Singapore	X	4. study English	√

1. I'm going to learn to ski.   **2.** _____

3. _____   **4.** _____

B. Look at David's diary for next week. Write correct answers as in the example.

David's Diary

Monday:	play volleyball
Tuesday:	play tennis
Wednesday:	study English
Thursday:	learn to swim
Friday:	go to a museum
Saturday:	go skiing

ex. Q: Is David going to play soccer next Monday?
    A: No, he isn't. He's going to play volleyball.

1. Q: Is David going to play tennis next Tuesday?
    A: _____

2. Q: Is David going to study Japanese next Wednesday?
    A: _____

3. Q: Is David going to go fishing next Saturday?
    A: _____

Super Speaking

● Look at the example and practice with a partner. Use the cues given. Then change roles and practice again.

Is Linda **going to** take the dog for a walk tomorrow?

No, she isn't. She's going to go shopping.

Linda / take the dog for a walk / tomorrow / ?
⇨ go shopping

Ava / take the school bus to school / tomorrow morning / ?
⇨ ride her bicycle to school

the children / watch TV / next Wednesday / ?
⇨ study math

they / travel by train / tomorrow / ?
⇨ go to the park

Building Vocabulary

A. Fill in the blanks with the correct words.

| fishing | yoga | the Internet | the guitar |
| rope | a musical instrument | a skateboard | to music |

1.

do _____

2.

jump _____

3.

surf _____

4.

play _____

5.

listen _____

6.

ride _____

7.

go _____

8.

play _____

27

B. Match the words and meanings. Draw a line between the word and its meaning.

WORD

MEANING

1.

free time

a. a building in which movies are shown

2.

movie theater

b. a board like a wide ski

3.

horror

c. time available for hobbies and other activities that you enjoy

4.

snowboard

d. a strong feeling of shock or fear

C. Circle the correct words and complete the sentences.

1.

He was a big _____ of the singer.

(pan / fan)

2.

We usually go _____ on the weekends.

(cycling / skiing)

3.

I'd like to be a _____ skateboarder.

(professor / professional)

4.

In the afternoon, I often go _____.

(rock climbing / scuba diving)

A. Put the activities into different categories.

cooking	going out with friends	listening to music / the radio
playing computer games	visiting friends or family	watching TV / a DVD
shopping	surfing the Internet	swimming

doing aerobics

Going Out	Staying at Home
doing aerobics	*cooking*

B. Imagine that you are applying for a job and that this is a part of your application form. Write a few sentences about your free-time activities. Use the words/phrases above.

Free-Time Activities

C. Make sentences using the information in the table below.

Adverbs	Name	Activities
always	**1.** Britney	watches TV after dinner
usually	**2.** Ben	studies for the tests on Saturday
often	**3.** Susan	cooks for her grandmother on the weekend
sometimes	**4.** Tom and Jane	play football with their cousins
never	**5.** Caroline	is bored with classes

1. *Britney always watches TV after dinner.*

2. _____

3. _____

4. _____

5. _____

Super Writing 1

A. What do you usually do in your free time? Write the sentences like the example.

1.

| go swimming | at the beach |

➡ I usually *go swimming at the beach*.

2.

| play tennis | at the tennis court |

➡ _____

3.

| go hiking | in the forest |

➡ _____

4.

| volunteer | at the nursing home |

➡ _____

B. Look at the pictures. Write the sentences using the phrases in the box.

| go to the movies / once a month | enjoy cycling / every day |
| plays soccer / once a week | does yoga / three times a week |

1.

The boy _____*plays soccer once a week*_____.

2.

We _____.

3.

Kathy _____.

4.

They _____.

1~3 Unscramble the words to make sentences.

4~7 Sentence Transformation. / N(Negative), Q(Question)

1.

| I | in my free time | . | usually enjoy | reading comic books |

⇨ _____

2.

| when I have some free time | , | listening to music | like | . | I |

⇨ _____

3.

| with my dad | to watch | international games | . | I | go |

⇨ _____

4.

I play basketball with my older brother. (N)

⇨ _____

5.

She plays the guitar. (Q)

⇨ _____

6.

He and she spend their free time differently. (Q)

⇨ _____

7.

She goes shopping once a week. (N)

⇨ _____

Super Speaking!

A. Listen to the dialog again. Please circle the correct words or write the missing words. 🔘 Track 30

Betty: ┃ (a) What / (b) Who ┃ do you do in your free time?

Eric: Well, I ____u____ play soccer for my school.

Betty: ┃ (a) How many / (b) How often ┃ do you play?

Eric: We play once a week, on Saturday afternoon.

Betty: Do you play other sports?

Eric: Yes, I do. I play ____b____ with my older brother.

Betty: Does he go to your school?

Eric: No, he ┃ (a) doesn't / (b) don't ┃. He goes to university. Do you play sports?

Betty: No, I don't.

Eric: What do you do in your free time?

Betty: I usually play the guitar.

Eric: That's cool! I'd love to ____l____ how to play the guitar someday.

Betty: I'd be happy ┃ (a) to teach / (b) teaching ┃ you.

Eric: Really? Thanks!

B. ┃Let's Talk┃ Ask and answer the questions about the dialog with your partner.

1. What does Eric do in his free time?
⇨ He usually _play soccer for his school_____.

2. When does Eric play soccer?
⇨ He plays it _____.

3. What does Betty do in her free time?
⇨ She _____.

4. Does Eric know how to play the guitar?
⇨ No, _____. He'd like to learn _____.

Grammar Focus 1

● **The Simple Present: Yes/No questions**

- Questions have *do* or *does* before the subject to make a yes/no question. We often use *do/don't* or *does/doesn't* in short answers to questions.

Q: Does Ava jog every morning?
A: Yes, she does.

Question

Do / Does	Subject	Base verb
Do	I / you / we / they	like ~?
Does	he / she / it / Tom, Mary..	

Answer

Yes, I/you/we/they do.	No, I/you/we/they don't.
Yes, he/she/it does.	No, he/she/it doesn't.

Grammar Focus 2

● **Adverbs of Frequency / How often ...? / Information Questions with What**

- Adverbs of frequency tell us how many times something happens. Adverbs of frequency go before the main verb but after the verb be.

- We use *how often* to ask about the frequency of an action.

- The question word *what* asks about specific information. (What + do/does + Subject + base verb ~?)

Q: How often does your father cook?
A: He always cooks.

Q: What do Kangaroos eat?
A: They eat plants.

always	–	usually	–	often	–	sometimes	–	seldom/hardly	–	never
(100%)		(about 90%)		(about 70%)		(about 50%)		(about 10%)		(0 %)

A. Add the adverbs of frequency in brackets.

1. I get up at 7 a.m. (always) ⇨ *I always get up at 7 a.m.*

2. I have breakfast at 7:30. (usually) ⇨ _____

3. I arrive late. (sometimes) ⇨ _____

4. She is in her office. (usually) ⇨ _____

B. Make questions and match them to their answers.

1. Tom drinks milk every day. *Does Tom drink milk every day?* • • Yes, she does.

2. Ann teaches French. _____ • • No, they don't.

3. Bob and Kevin play baseball. _____ • • Yes, he does.

C. Read and make questions.

1.    2.    3.    4.

1. Q: *What does she like?*
   A: She likes pizza.

2. Q: _____ ?
   A: She has a puppy.

3. Q: _____ ?
   A: He wants the car.

4. Q: _____ ?
   A: They have lunch.

Super Speaking

● Work with a partner. Taking turns, ask and answer questions as in the example.

Student A: Imagine that you are a reporter and that you're doing a survey on people's free-time activities. Interview Student B and complete the form.

Student B: Student A is interviewing you about your free-time activities. Answer his/her questions.

A: Do you play sports?
B: Yes, I do.
A: What sport(s) do you play?
B: I play ...

What do you do in your free time?		
play sports?	Yes ☐	No ☐
What sport(s) ...?		
like listening to music?	Yes ☐	No ☐
What kind of music ...?		
watch movies?	Yes ☐	No ☐
What kind of movie ...?		
play a musical instrument?	Yes ☐	No ☐
What musical instrument ...?		
like books?	Yes ☐	No ☐
What kind of book ...?		

Building Vocabulary

A. Look and check the correct words.

1.

orange juice _____

coffee _____

2.

watermelon _____

apple _____

3.

pizza _____

hamburger _____

4.

meat _____

wheat _____

5.

doughnuts _____

vegetables _____

6.

green tea _____

Coke _____

B. Circle the correct words and fill in the blanks.

1.

I have lunch at the _____, at one o'clock.

(cafeteria / library)

2.

There's also _____ for dessert.

(Fish and chips / chocolate cake)

3.

_____ and doughnuts are popular all over the world.

(French fries / Sandwiches)

C. Match the words and meanings. Draw a line between the word and its meaning.

WORD

MEANING

1.

food

2.

healthy

3.

architect

4.

meal

a. someone whose job is to design buildings

b. an occasion when you eat, especially breakfast, lunch, or dinner

c. strong and well in your body

d. things that you eat

D. Let's Talk Practice the conversation with your partner using the words under the pictures.

1.
A: Where do you usually go out for dinner?

B: ____McDonald's____. That place is famous for its ____hamburgers____.

a.

McDonald's / hamburgers

b.

Pizza Hut / pizzas

2.
A: How much do ____French fries____ cost there?

B: Around $8.

a.

French fries

b.

noodles

A. Read an article about healthy and unhealthy foods.

BE HEALTHY!

Do you eat healthy food for breakfast, lunch and dinner? It's important. Apples, watermelon and grapes are healthy, but too much ice cream is unhealthy. I love carrots and potatoes. They are healthy, but French fries are not healthy.

Now, answer the questions.

1. Q: Is watermelon healthy?　　　　A: _Yes, it is._

2. Q: Are French fries unhealthy?　　　A: _____

3. Q: Are carrots unhealthy?　　　　　A: _____

4. Q: Are potatoes healthy?　　　　　A: _____

5. Q: Are grapes and apples healthy?　A: _____

B. What do you eat for breakfast, lunch and dinner?

I have breakfast at 7:30. I eat _____

_____

_____

C. Cathy is in a restaurant. Put the waiter's words and Cathy's answers in the correct order.

Waiter　　　　　to / ready / you / Are / order / ?

1. _Are you ready to order?_

Cathy　　　　　Yes, / a burger / I / have / will

2. _____

Waiter　　　　　you like / would / What kind of burger / ?

3. _____

Cathy　　　　　the bacon cheeseburger / would / I / like

4. _____

Super Writing 1

A. Look at the pictures. Write sentences as in the example.

1.

| pizza | an Italian dish |

⇨ My favorite food is pizza. Pizza is an Italian dish.

2.

| sushi | a Japanese dish |

⇨ _____

3.

| crepe | a French dish |

⇨ _____

4.

| kimchi | a Korean traditional dish |

⇨ _____

5.

| bulgogi | a Korean dish |

⇨ _____

6.

| taco | a Mexican dish |

⇨ _____

7.

| a hamburger | an American dish |

⇨ _____

Super Writing 2

● 1~4 Unscramble the words to make sentences.
● 5~6 Sentence Transformation. / N(Negative), Q(Question)

1.

breakfast | I | at | have | seven-thirty | .

⇨ _____

2.

are | all over the world | . | popular | sandwiches and doughnuts

⇨ _____

3.

a Mexican traditional dish | . | are | Mexican tacos

⇨ _____

4.

how often | ? | eat | do | at fast-food restaurant | you

⇨ _____

5.

Apples, watermelons and grapes are healthy. (Q)

⇨ _____

6.

People eat fruit in various ways. (N)

⇨ _____

Super Speaking!

A. Listen to the dialog again. Please circle the correct words or write the missing words. 🔘 Track 39

Waiter: Good evening. What can I get you?

Customer: Um, I'm not _____r_____ to order yet.

              | (a) Will / (b) Can | I have a minute or two?

Waiter: Certainly. Take your time.

              ....

Waiter: Can I take your _____o_____ now?

Customer: Yes, I think so. I'd | (a) like / (b) alike | vegetable soup to start with.

Waiter: And for the main course?

Customer: I'd like a burger.

Waiter: What _____k_____ of burger would you like?

Customer: What do you _____r_____, the double cheeseburger or the bacon cheeseburger?

Waiter: | (a) Either / (b) Both | are good, but I prefer the bacon cheeseburger.

Customer: Okay, I'd like the bacon cheeseburger.

Waiter: Would you like _____a_____ to drink?

Customer: I'd like a bottle of mineral water, please.

Waiter: Thank you.

B. [Let's Talk] Read and repeat the dialog. Then use the speaking cards to practice it with your partner.

A: Do you like ❶_____bananas_____.

B: Yes, I do. They're tasty.

A: Do you eat ❷_____mushrooms_____?

B: No, I think they're horrible. What about you?

A: I like ❷_____mushrooms_____ a lot. They're good for you, too.

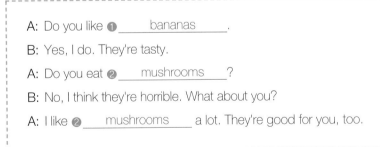

❶ carrots
❷ onions

❶ strawberries
❷ potatoes

A/An & Some

Grammar Focus

A/An & Some

- *A/an* shows that we are talking about *one* person or thing. We use *an* before a vowel sound (for example, the normal sound of a, e, i, o, u).

- We use *some* to say the amount when we don't know how much. We use *some* with both uncountable nouns (e.g. sugar, bread, etc.) and plural countable nouns (e.g. pens, cars, etc.). *Some* means a little or a few. We use *some* in positive statements.

A dog is an animal.

A parrot is a bird.

There is an apple and there is some water.

	Countable Nouns	Uncountable Nouns
a / an	a fork an orange	water milk
some	some forks some apples	some water some milk

A. Write *a*, *an* or *some*.

1.

_____ ant

2.

_____ cheese

3.

_____ bread

4.

_____ juice

5.

_____ guitar

6.

_____ elephant

41

B. What is there in the refrigerator? Write sentences.

1. Fruit?　　　　Yes, *there is some fruit.*

2. Apples?　　　Yes, *there are some apples.*

3. Milk?　　　　Yes, _____

4. Butter?　　　Yes, _____

5. Vegetables?　Yes, _____

6. Tomatoes?　　Yes, _____

7. Meat?　　　　Yes, _____

C. Look at the pictures and complete the dialogs with *a*, *an* or *some*.

1.

A: Are you hungry?

B: Not really. Can I have _____ apple and _____ water, please?

A: Sure.

2. A: Here are _____ carrots, broccoli and _____ tomato for the salad, mom.

B: OK, put them on the table.

Super Speaking

• Work with a partner. Andrew, Betty, Dot and Fred are eating. There's some cheese, some eggs, some salad and some fruit. Who has what?

Andrew has some cheese, some salad and some fruit, but he doesn't have any eggs.

	cheese	eggs	salad	fruit
Andrew	✓	✗	✓	✓
Betty	✓	✓	✓	✗
Dot	✓	✓	✗	✓
Fred	✗	✓	✓	✗

Your turn now!

Building Vocabulary

A. Look and check (√) the correct words.

1.

dress _____
T-shirt _____

2.

sneakers _____
boots _____

3.

sun hat _____
bag _____

4.

blouse _____
swimsuit _____

5.

short-sleeved shirt _____
sweatshirt _____

6.

a pair of socks _____
a pair of sneakers _____

B. Choose and fill in the blanks to make sentences.

| wear | medium | shopping | size |

1.

Do you like _____ for clothes?

2.

What _____ is this jumper?

3.

I usually _____ some trainers.

4.

These are small and they're too tight.
Do you have a _____?

C. Check the meaning of the words in bold and answer the questions.

a gift shop   a dry-cleaner's   a hairdresser's   a bakery

a butcher's   a post office   a clothes shop   a pharmacy

1. Where can you take your **clothes** when they're **dirty**?   ⇨   _____a dry-cleaner's_____

2. Where can you **have a haircut**?   ⇨   _____

3. Where do they **sell bread and cakes**?   ⇨   _____

4. Where can you **get** a **present** for a friend?   ⇨   _____

5. Where do you **post letters** and **parcels**?   ⇨   _____

6. Where can you buy **toothpaste** and **medicine**?   ⇨   _____

7. Where can you go for new **T-shirts**?   ⇨   _____

8. Where can you **buy some meat**?   ⇨   _____

D. Refer to the definitions and complete the sentences.

• leather	n. animal skins used for making things such as shoes and belts
• customer	n. a person or company that buys goods or services
• change	n. money that you get back when you pay too much for something

1. I gave him a dollar and he gave me 30 cents in _____.

2. I can't believe how expensive this _____ bag is!

3. This lot is for _____ parking only.

A. Work with your partner. Look at the questions. Circle **S** if the question is asked by the store clerk. Circle **C** if the question is asked by the customer.

1. Can I try this on?   **S**   **(C)**

2. Can I help you?   **S**   **C**

3. I think these are too big. Do you have a smaller pair?   **S**   **C**

4. They really are nice. How much is this one?   **S**   **C**

5. Do you have it in a different color?   **S**   **C**

6. Yes, I see. Well, I'll exchange this for you.   **S**   **C**

B. Number the sentences to make a conversation.

_____1_____ Can I help you?

_____ I'll take it.

_____ It's seven dollars.

_____ How much is this dress?

_____ Here's your dress.

_____ You're welcome.

_____ Thank you.

C. Match the questions with the answers.

1. How much does this wallet cost?   •   • a. They are ten dollars.

2. How much are these shoes?   •   • b. They're dark blue.

3. What color are those socks?   •   • c. It's five dollars.

4. What size are these sneakers?   •   • d. The wallet costs eight dollars.

5. How much is it?   •   • e. They're size 42.

Super Writing 1

A. Look at the picture and make sentences like the example.

1.

bag	$7

A: How much is this bag?

B: It's seven dollars including tax.

2.

T-shirt	$5

A: _____

B: _____

3.

sun hat	$9

A: _____

B: _____

4.

blouse	$12

A: _____

B: _____

5.

sweater	$15

A: _____

B: _____

B. Look at the pictures. Write the sentences using the phrases in the box.

> by credit card   window shopping   in the bookstore

1.

The customer is

_____ .

2.

The woman wants to pay

_____ .

3.

Is _____

a total waste of time?

- 1~3 Unscramble the words to make sentences.
- 4~7 Sentence Transformation. / N(Negative) Q(Question)

1.

| I'm | a dress | . | looking | for |

⇨ _____

2.

| a leather jacket | . | I | would like |

⇨ _____

3.

| It | on every lady | . | good | looks | really |

⇨ _____

4.

Customers are talking to salespeople in a store. (Q)

⇨ _____

5.

The price is what. (Q)

⇨ _____

6.

The students are waiting for a bus. (N)

⇨ _____

7.

You like going shopping in other countries. (Q)

⇨ _____

Super Speaking!

A. Listen to the dialog again. Please circle the correct words or write the missing words. ⊙ Track 46

Shop assistant: May I help you with │ (a) something / (b) anything │?

Customer: Yes, I'd like a leather jacket, please.
Have you got any _____b_____ jackets?

Shop assistant: Of course. This jacket is very popular.
It does look very nice on you.

Customer: Yes, but │ (a) don't / (b) do │ you think it's _____a_____ ?

Shop assistant: What size are you?

Customer: Do you have it in a _____l_____ ?

Shop assistant: Here you are.

Customer: It's cool! How │ (a) many / (b) much │ is it?

Shop assistant: It's on sale. Let's see... It's $99.

Customer: It's too expensive for me.

Shop assistant: But it's a nice jacket, sir.

Customer: You're right. I'll take it. Here's $100.

Shop assistant: Thank you very much and here's your _____c_____ .

Customer: Thanks.

B. Let's Talk Complete the Key Expressions with words from the dialog.

Key Expressions: Shopping

SHOP ASSISTANT		CUSTOMER
Can I help you?	⇨	Yes, I'm looking for ❶ _____.
What about this one?	⇨	Don't you think it's ❷ _____?
What size are you?	⇨	❸ _____.
Here you are.		
It's ❹ _____.	⇦	How much is it?
Thank you and here's your ❻ _____.	⇦	❺ _____. Here's $100.

Grammar Focus 1

● **Present Progressive**

- We use the present progressive to talk about activities happening right now. We form the present progressive with a present form of *to be(am, is, are)* and *-ing* form.

Olivia is sitting on the sofa.
She is watching a scary movie.

Subject	Be verb	Base verb + v-ing
I	am	
He / She / It	is	walking.
You / We / They	are	

Base verb + -ing	One vowel + consonant	Verb + e + -ing
talk ⇨ talking	sit ⇨ sitting	come ⇨ coming
walk ⇨ walking	swim ⇨ swimming	dance ⇨ dancing
drink ⇨ drinking	run ⇨ running	make ⇨ making
sleep ⇨ sleeping	get ⇨ getting	write ⇨ writing

Grammar Focus 2

● **One / Ones**

- We use the pronoun *one* when we don't want to repeat a singular countable noun that has already been mentioned.

- We use the pronoun *ones* when we don't want to repeat a plural countable noun that has already been mentioned.

A: Which bag is yours?
B: The blue one.

Those aren't my sunglasses.
The ones on the desk are mine.

The white dress is OK, but
I like the pink one better.

49

A. Rewrite the sentences using the *Present Progressive*.

1.

She plays the violin.

⇨ *She is playing the violin.*

2.

They paint the house.

⇨ _____

3.

Nancy wears black shoes.

⇨ _____

4.

He does his homework.

⇨ _____

B. Complete the sentences with *one* or *ones*.

1. Do you have an idea? – Yes, I have ___one___.

2. Which is your car? – The black _____.

3. Which jeans fit you better? –The black _____.

4. Which books are yours? – The _____ on the table.

Super Speaking

● Work with a partner. Choose a picture from the ones below but don't tell your partner. Take turns to ask and answer questions to find out which person your partner has chosen.

50

Everyday Activities

Building Vocabulary

A. Choose and fill in the blanks to make sentences.

yoga	washes the dishes	homework	plane
takes a shower	breakfast	feeds	gets up

1.

I'm doing my _____.

2.

Did you have _____ today?

3.

Kathy _____ at 6:30 every morning.

4.

After dinner, she sometimes _____.

5.

He always _____ before he has breakfast.

6.

They're sitting on a _____.

7.

The girls are learning _____.

8.

Nancy always _____ the animals before she has breakfast.

B. Read the definitions. Cross out (X) the unnecessary letters and write the correct words.

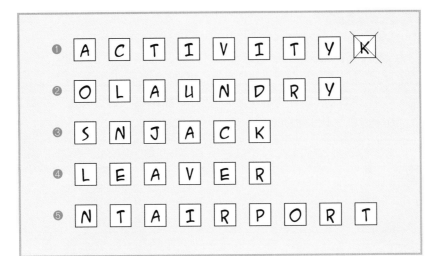

1. when people are moving around, doing things ⇨ _____activity_____

2. the dirty clothes and sheets which need to be, are being or have been washed ⇨ _____

3. a small amount of food that you eat between meals ⇨ _____

4. to go away from someone or something, for a short time or permanently ⇨ _____

5. a place that airplanes arrive at and leave from ⇨ _____

C. Check the correct phrases for each picture.

1.

_____ watching TV

_____ making dinner

2.

_____ doing the laundry

_____ doing the house work

3.

_____ reading a book

_____ playing the violin

4.

_____ study in the library

_____ have lunch

5.

_____ read a book

_____ talk on the phone

6.

_____ ride the horse

_____ feed the horse

A. Look at the daily routine and complete the sentences as in the example.

1.

get up

Amy _____gets up at seven_____ in the morning.

2.

have breakfast

She _____.

3.

go to school

She _____.

4.

eat lunch

She _____.

5.

finish school

She _____.

6.

do her homework

She _____.

B. Match to make sentences.

1. Kevin and Jack are watching   a. a cake?

2. Is Mom making   b. a movie on television.

3. What book are you   c. their homework.

4. Tom and Lisa are doing   d. on the telephone?

5. Is your sister talking   e. reading?

Super Writing 1

A. Use the expressions in the box to write sentences about your daily activities. Draw the times on the clocks.

get up	get dressed	eat breakfast	brush my teeth
leave for school	get to school	have lunch	start lessons
eat dinner	watch TV	talk to my friends on the phone	help my mother
do my homework	use my computer	read books	go to bed

1.

I always ___get up___

___at 7 o'clock___.

2.

I usually _____

_____.

3.

I never _____

_____.

4.

I sometimes _____

_____.

5.

I often _____

_____.

6.

I always _____

_____.

B. Use the *present progressive* to make two sentences about each situation, one negative and one affirmative.

1. Sunny: (watch TV) (play the drums)

Sunny isn't watching TV. She is playing the drums.

2. Jane: (read a newspaper) (sleep on the sofa)

_____

3. Bob: (talking on the phone) (jog in the park)

_____

Super Writing 2

● 1~3 Unscramble the words to make sentences.
● 4~7 Sentence Transformation. / N(Negative), Q(Question)

1.

every morning   .   at 6:30   she   gets up

⇨ _____

2.

always   at nine thirty   I   .   go to bed

⇨ _____

3.

in the afternoon   we   .   our homework   do

⇨ _____

4.

The man is reading a book. (Q)

⇨ _____

5.

She is waiting at the airport. (Q)

⇨ _____

6.

They are having lunch at the cafeteria. (N)

⇨ _____

7.

He is listening to K-pop music. (N)

⇨ _____

Super Speaking!

A. Listen to the dialog again. Please circle the correct words or write the missing words. ⊙ Track 54

Mum: Jennifer, you've got [(a) homework / (b) home page] and then it's time for bed.

Jennifer: Oh, Mum. It's not. This is my favorite ___p_____.

Mum: But it is eight o'clock.

Jennifer: Mum, I always ____g_____ at nine thirty, and I read in bed [(a) during / (b) until]
            ten o'clock.

Mum: You go to bed at nine [(a) thirteen / (b) thirty] at the weekend.
            You go to bed at nine o'clock on school days.

Jennifer: But Mum....

Mum: That's enough, Jennifer. You've got school tomorrow. Good-night!

Jennifer: But Mum, I ____h_____ school tomorrow. Tomorrow is Saturday!

B. Let's Talk Draw lines to match the places to the activities. Choose an activity and then have
a conversation with your partner.

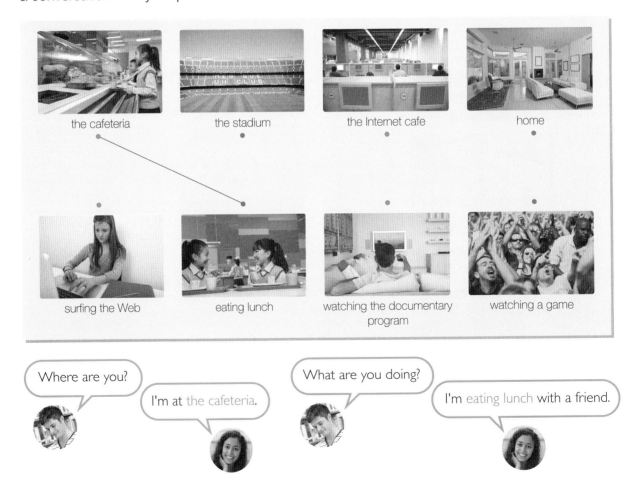

the cafeteria   the stadium   the Internet cafe   home

surfing the Web   eating lunch   watching the documentary   watching a game
                                                    program

Where are you?   What are you doing?

I'm at the cafeteria.   I'm eating lunch with a friend.

Grammar Focus 1

● **Present Progressive: negative statements & yes / no questions**

- To form the negative of the present progressive, we add *not* after the verb *be*.

- The verb *be* is placed before the subject to make a yes/no question in present progressive.

It isn't snowing. (= It's not snowing.)
It is raining.

Q: Is Karen eating an apple?
A: No, she isn't. She is eating a banana.

Grammar Focus 2

● **When/What Time**

- We use *when* and *what time* to ask about time. We use *at* for times of the day and for the expression at night.

Q: What time/When does the plane arrive?
A: The plane arrives at six-fifteen.

Question word	Do(es)	Subject	Base verb
When	do	you	
What time	does	(s)he	go to bed?

A. Look and make questions.

1.

the teacher / help students

Q: Is the teacher helping
   students?

2.

Nancy / sleep in the bed

Q: _____

_____

3.

they / walk to school

Q: _____

_____

57

B. Make questions as in the example.

1. A: *When/What time do you get up?*

    B: At 7:00. (I get up at 7:00 in the morning.)

2. A: _____

    B: At 8:45. (They get to school at eight forty-five.)

3. A: _____

    B: At 8:30. (Steve leaves for school at eight thirty.)

4. A: _____

    B: 9:00. (The movie starts at nine o'clock.)

5. A: _____

    B: Around 10:00. (I usually go to bed around ten o'clock.)

6. A: _____

    B: At 7:30. (The bus arrives at seven thirty.)

Super Speaking

● Look at the example and practice with a partner. Use the words below or invent your own.
(Then change roles and practice again.)

Olivia / eat dinner / ?
No ➪ read a book

Is Olivia eating dinner?

No, she isn't. She is reading a book.

they / wash the car / ?
No ➪ paint the house

the girl / take a shower / ?
No ➪ take a picture

the woman / work on her
computer / ?
No ➪ talk on her phone

Building Vocabulary

A. Choose and fill in the blanks to make sentences.

bone	headache	meal	medicine
stomachache	toothache	exercise	overweight

1.

Do you have a _____ ?

2.

Have some vegetables or some fruit in every _____ .

3.

I'm _____, so I really want to lose weight.

4.

My _____ is caused by stress.

5.

Take this _____ every night.

6.

Do you _____ regularly?

7.

I had a _____ on Friday night.

8.

Have you ever had an operation or broken a _____ ?

B. Read the definitions. Cross out (X) the unnecessary letters and write the correct words.

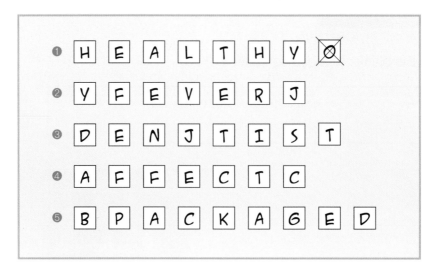

① H E A L T H Y ~~Ø~~

② Y F E V E R J

③ D E N J T I S T

④ A F F E C T C

⑤ B P A C K A G E D

1. strong and well in your body ⇨ <u>healthy</u>

2. an illness which causes an increase in how hot your body is ⇨ _____

3. someone whose job is to examine and treat people's teeth ⇨ _____

4. to produce a change in someone or something ⇨ _____

5. something wrapped in paper so that you can put it into the mail ⇨ _____

C. Check the correct phrases for each picture.

1.

_____ have a digital camera
_____ have a big meal

2.

_____ take a shower
_____ take some medicine

3.

_____ go hiking
_____ go bowling

4.

_____ worry about my weight
_____ worry about my height

A. Circle the best advice for these health problems.

1. I have a toothache.

   You should (have a hot drink / go to the dentist).

2. Jane has a cold.

   She should (get some sleep / listen to rock music).

3. He has a sore leg.

   He should (exercise / take it easy).

B. Tell this teenager what he *should* or *shouldn't* do.

1. He skips breakfast.
   ⇨ *He shouldn't skip breakfast.*

2. He comes home late.
   ⇨ _____

3. He doesn't do his homework.
   ⇨ _____

4. He doesn't listen to his parents.
   ⇨ _____

5. He doesn't listen in class.
   ⇨ _____

6. He doesn't clean his room.
   ⇨ _____

7. He asks for money from his parents every day.
   ⇨ _____

8. He's not nice to his brother and sister.
   ⇨ _____

9. He doesn't help with the housework.
   ⇨ _____

Super Writing 1

A. Read the conversation. Write T for true or F for false. Then correct the false sentences.

> Bob: Hey, Peter. How are you?
>
> Peter: Not too good. I'm not feeling well.
>
> Bob: What's wrong with you?
>
> Peter: I have a sore throat, a cough and I think I'm getting a fever.
>
> Bob: Did you take anything?
>
> Peter: Yes, I took some medicine.
>
> Bob: You should take it easy.
>
> Peter: I know, but I have to play soccer.
>
> Bob: Don't go! You should stay home tonight.

1. ____F____   Peter has sore feet and a sore arm.

   Peter has a sore throat, a cough and a fever.

2. _____   Bob took some medicine.

   _____

3. _____   Peter has to play soccer.

   _____

4. _____   Bob thinks Peter should see a dentist tonight.

   _____

B. Look at the pictures and make sentences as in the example.

1.
   a toothache   go to a dentist

   A: What's wrong with Susan?
   B: *She has got a toothache. She should go to a dentist.*

2.
   a headache   take an aspirin

   A: What's wrong with William?
   B: _____

3.
   a sore throat   have a hot drink

   A: What's wrong with Sarah?
   B: _____

● 1~3 Unscramble the words to make sentences.
● 4~7 Sentence Transformation. / N(Negative), Q(Question)

1.

junk food | . | a lot of | teenagers | eat

⇨ _____

2.

overweight | are | . | many young people

⇨ _____

3.

. | go hiking | I | on the weekends

⇨ _____

4.

You should eat fried food. (N)

⇨ _____

5.

Sarah took a painkiller. (Q)

⇨ _____

6.

Lisa has got a black cat. (Q)

⇨ _____

7.

Sarah could go to the library because of an earache. (N)

⇨ _____

Super Speaking!

A. Listen to the dialog again. Please circle the correct words or write the missing words. ⊙ Track 63

Eric: Hi, Sarah. Where ☐ (a) are / (b) were ☐ you last Saturday? You didn't come to the library.

Sarah: Hi! I really wanted to, but I ___c_____ .

Eric: Why? What was the matter with you?

Sarah: I had a ☐ (a) headache / (b) toothache ☐ on Friday night and I couldn't sleep all night.

Eric: Did you take a painkiller?

Sarah: Yes, I did. But it didn't work, so I had to go to the dentist's.

My tooth was ___d_____ and he had to pull it out.

Eric: Poor you! Did it ☐ (a) hunt / (b) hurt ☐?

Sarah: Of course, it did. I could only drink some water. I couldn't speak for some time.

Eric: Oh, no! How do you ☐ (a) feel / (b) felt ☐ now?

Sarah: I am ___f_____ , thanks. I should go now. See you tomorrow.

Eric: See you.

B. Let's Talk Work with a partner. Use the prompts to give advice about the health problems.

Should / Have(Has) Got

Grammar Focus 1

● Should & Shouldn't

- We use *should* to give advice to someone and to say that something is a good idea.

- We use *shouldn't* to say that something is not good idea.

Maria has a terrible headache.

She should go to bed early.

She shouldn't listen to loud music.

Grammar Focus 2

● Have (Got) and Has (Got)

- We use *have (got)* and *has (got)* to show that something belongs to somebody, to describe people, animals or things, or to express a temporary state.

- We usually use *have got* and *has got* in conversations or in letters and e-mails to friends. *Have got* has the same meaning as *have*.

Nancy has got a fever.

She has got long black hair.

have		has	
I / We		He	
You	have got a daughter.	She	has got a problem.
They		It	

∗ When we talk about something that happens repeatedly, we do not use *have(has) got*. We prefer to use *have* with *do/does* in the negative and interrogative.

I often have headaches.   She doesn't usually have an earache.

I've got a headache now.   She hasn't got an earache.

A. Complete the sentences with *have got* or *has got* as in the example.

1. Jim _____ has got _____ a guitar.

2. Henry and I _____ new sunglasses.

3. That man _____ a new car.

4. Mary _____ two brothers.

B. Complete the blanks with *should* or *shouldn't*.

1. Tom has had the flu for two weeks now! He _____ should _____ see a doctor.

2. People _____ hunt the cheetah because. It's an endangered species.

3. A: I need to lose weight. What _____ I do?

   B: You _____ join an aerobics class. It's great way to keep fit.

4. Brian looks exhausted. He _____ work so hard.

5. Ava coundn't sleep well last night. She _____ drink coffee.

6. A: My parents don't give me enough pocket money.

   B: You _____ find a part-time job then.

● Look at the example and practice with a partner. Use the words below or invent your own.
(Then change roles and practice again.)

Has Cindy got black hair?

No, she hasn't. She's got brown hair.

Cindy / black hair / ?
No ⇨ brown hair

Tina / green eyes / ?
No ⇨ blue eyes

Kevin / an MP3 player / ?
No ⇨ a smartphone

Karen and Tiffany / notebooks / ?
No ⇨ cups

School Life

Building Vocabulary

A. Look and check the correct words.

1.

art _____

math _____

2.

history _____

science _____

3.

English _____

geography _____

4.

geography _____

literature _____

5.

math _____

physical education _____

6.

music _____

social studies _____

B. Circle the correct words and fill in the blanks.

1.

The school _____ at 9 a.m.

(starts / ends)

2.

_____ the 4th class in the morning, I have lunch

(Before / After)

with my friends in the cafeteria.

3.

I'm usually very _____ by the end of the week.

(tired / happy)

C. Match the words and meanings. Draw a line between the word and its meaning.

WORD

MEANING

1.

different

a. to do something for someone

2.

grade

b. all the things that happened
   in the past

3.

help

c. not the same

4.

history

d. not interesting or exciting

5.

boring

e. to take someone or
   something to a place or
   someone

6.

bring

f. a letter or number that shows
   how well you did in school

A. Unscramble the words to make a conversation.

1. A: your / What's / subject / favorite / ?   ⇨ A: _____

2. B: subject / My / favorite / English / is / .   ⇨ B: _____

3. A: English / Why / like / you / do / ?   ⇨ A: _____

4. B: my / like / English like / teacher / Because / I / .   ⇨ B: _____

5. A: in / math / , / you / Are / interested / too / ?   ⇨ A: _____

6. B: am / , / Yes / I / .   ⇨ B: _____

B. Read, guess and say what subjects are these? Which of them do you study?

1. This language is spoken in Great Britain, the USA and many other countries. It is studied at school too.

⇨ _____

2. This subject helps our bodies to be strong and healthy. It is held in the gym at school or at the stadium.

⇨ _____

3. This subject is about the countries, oceans, mountains, climate, seas, rivers and cities. It is very interesting.

⇨ _____

4. This subject is about the historical events happened in our country and abroad long years ago.

⇨ _____

5. This subject is about the numbers, different actions; addition, subtraction, division, multiplication.

⇨ _____

Super Writing 1

A. Read about Jenny and write five things you like and don't like to do.

Jenny likes many things. She thinks physical education is interesting, but she doesn't like badminton or tennis. She likes volleyball. Jenny also likes Korean. She is interested in Korean culture and the traditional lifestyle of Korean people. She likes music, too. She listens to loud rock music when she studies. She likes to sing and play the guitar. Jenny also likes dancing.

Like to do	Don't like to do

B. Look at the example. Make the conversations as in the example.

1.

math	physical education

A: _Are you interested in math?_

B: No, I'm not.

A: What's your favorite subject, then?

B: _I like physical education._

2.

history	math

A: _____

B: No, I'm not.

A: What's your favorite subject, then?

B: _____

3.

geography	music

A: _____

B: No, I'm not.

A: What's your favorite subject, then?

B: _____

Super Writing 2

- 1~3 Unscramble the words to make sentences.
- 4~7 Sentence Transformation. / N(Negative), Q(Question), T(Tense)

1.

| starts | at 9 a.m. | the school |

⇨ _____

2.

| in the cafeteria | I | . | with my friends | have lunch |

⇨ _____

3.

| I | don't have to get up early | don't have classes | . | I | because |

⇨ _____

4.

He has to clean up after class. (Q)

⇨ _____

5.

They must bring their cell phones to school. (N)

⇨ _____

6.

Do you get a good grade in the test? (T - Past)

⇨ _____

7.

They go to different rooms for different classes. (Q)

⇨ _____

Super Speaking!

A. Listen to the conversation between two students. Then, answer the questions. While you listen, you can take notes. (●) Track **72**

Listening Notes

	Prepare ●••	Speak ●••
1. Do the boy and the girl have to wear school uniforms?	(5 seconds)	(10 seconds)
2. Can the boy bring his cell phone to school?	(5 seconds)	(10 seconds)
3. What do they have to do after class?	(5 seconds)	(10 seconds)

B. Let's Talk Look at the example and practice with a partner. Use the words below or invent your own. (Then change roles and practice again.)

social studies / ?
⇨ get up early to study

How do you study for your social studies exam?

I usually get up early to study.

math / ?
⇨ solve a lot of exercises

geography / ?
⇨ stay up late to study

English / ?
⇨ study by working with a group

Grammar Focus 1

● **Can: permission**

- We use *can* to give permission. We use *can't* to refuse permission.

- We use *Can I~?* to ask for permission to do something.

You can use this phone, but you can't make a long distance call.

Can I ask a question, please?

Grammar Focus 2

● **Must**

- We use *must* to say that something is very important or necessary. We often use *must* for rules or strong advice. We use *must not(= mustn't)* when something is against the law or rules or it isn't right.

We must listen to the teacher.

You mustn't go near the fire. It's dangerous.

A. Make sentences with *you can* in these situations.

1. You have a dictionary. Your friend wants to see it for a minute.

You say: ⇨   *You can see my dictionary for a minute.*

2. You have a digital camera. Your friend wants to take a picture with it.

You say: ⇨ _____

3. You have a calculator. Your friend wants to use it for a minute.

You say: ⇨ _____

B. Make sentences using *must* or *mustn't*.

1.

not swim / in the lake

⇨ You mustn't swim in the lake.

2.

not speak / in class

⇨ _____

3.

exercise / for your health

⇨ _____

4.

not use / your mobile / in class

⇨ _____

Super Speaking

● Look at the example and practice with a partner. Use the words below or invent your own. (Then change roles and practice again.)

drink / a glass of water / ?
⇨ Of course

Can I drink a glass of water?

Of course. Here it is.

Thank you.

borrow / your MP3 player / ?
⇨ Certainly

use / your pencil / ?
⇨ No problem

borrow / your pencil sharpener / ?
⇨ Sure

Special Days

Building Vocabulary

A. Choose and fill in the blanks to make sentences.

Thanksgiving	pray	custom	birthday
pick up	stethoscope	party	foreigners

1.

My _____ is on October tenth.

2.

I usually meet my friends and have a birthday _____.

3.

It is a _____ handed down to us from ancient times.

4.

She has continued to _____ for us all these days.

5.

I could _____ some fresh produce for dinner.

6.

The doctor examined her with a _____.

7.

Korean seems to be afraid of meeting _____.

8.

_____ is one of America's most important holidays.

B. Look and check the correct words.

1.

parents _____

grandparents _____

2.

arrow _____

yarn _____

3.

August _____

April _____

4.

general _____

scholar _____

5.

Valentine's Day _____

Halloween _____

6.

scary _____

funny _____

C. Match the words and meanings. Draw a line between the word and its meaning.

WORD

MEANING

1.

meaning

a. different

2.

believe

b. to have a special meal or party because of a particular event

3.

various

c. The meaning of words, sings, or actions is what they represent of show.

4.

celebrate

d. to think that something is true

A. Complete the three conversations. Choose (a), (b) or (c).

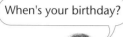

When's your birthday?

(a) My birthday is on November 11th.
(b) I'm 15 years old.
(c) Today is Tuesday, the fourteenth of February.

1. When is Korean's Independent day?

(a) It is Sunday.

(b) It is on August 15th.

(c) How do you celebrate it?

2. What's your favorite festival?

(a) It's on the first day of January.

(b) People play music and we dance.

(c) Well, I love Halloween.

3. What do you eat at Christmas?

(a) Ham, potatoes, and apple pie.

(b) We go to church and then have dinner.

(c) I like Chinese New Year.

B. Read the text and fill in the calendar.

March is a very busy month! Independence Movement is the first day of March. There are English tests on March 8th and March 17th. Our class play is on March 4th. It's a part of Arts Festival. It's on the 4th and 5th. We have a class trip on March 21st and soccer game on March 30th.

March

Sunday	Monday	Tuesday	Wednesday	Thursday	Friday	Saturday
					1	2
3	4	5	6	7	English Test 8	9
10	11	12	13	14	15	16
English Test 17	18	19	20	21	22	23
24	25	26	27	28	29	30
31						

Super Writing 1

A. Look at the pictures and write what Olivia usually does on her birthday.

| make a birthday cake | have a party | play the violin | open presents with his friends |

Brian usually makes a birthday cake on his birthday. He has a party with his friends. He plays the violin and he opens presents with his friends.

1.

2.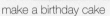

3.

4.

| make party hats | have a big party | play the guitar | get birthday presents |

Olivia usually _____

_____

_____

_____

B. Answer the questions.

1. What's the date today?

_____

2. When's your father's birthday?

_____

3. When's your mother's birthday?

_____

4. When's your best friend's birthday?

_____

● 1~3 Unscramble the words to make sentences.
● 4~7 Sentence Transformation. / N(Negative), Q(Question), T(Tense)

1.

| on your birthday | ? | do | what do you | usually |

⇨ _____

2.

| Korean traditional custom | . | is | Doljanchi | a |

⇨ _____

3.

| on a special table | . | parents | various items | put |

⇨ _____

4.

They want her to be a scholar. (Q)

⇨ _____

5.

My birthday is on November 11th. (N)

⇨ _____

6.

I go to the movies with my family. (T-Past)

⇨ _____

7.

Peter wants to go to college to study economics. (Q)

⇨ _____

Super Speaking!

A. Listen to the conversation between two students. Then, answer the questions. While you listen, you can take notes. ⊙ Track 85

Listening Notes

	Prepare ●••	Speak ●••
1. When is Halloween?	(5 seconds)	(10 seconds)
2. Why do young children go from door to door?	(5 seconds)	(10 seconds)
3. Why do children wear costumes as ghosts or monsters?	(5 seconds)	(10 seconds)
4. What does the girl do on New Year's Day?	(5 seconds)	(10 seconds)

B. Let's Talk Look at the example and practice with a partner. Use the words below or invent your own. (Then change roles and practice again.)

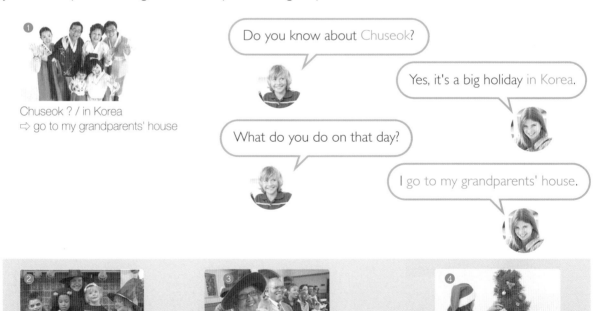

Chuseok ? / in Korea
⇨ go to my grandparents' house

Do you know about Chuseok?

Yes, it's a big holiday in Korea.

What do you do on that day?

I go to my grandparents' house.

Halloween ? / in Britain
⇨ go to a Halloween party

Easter ? / in Europe
⇨ go to church and then have dinner

Christmas ? / in Korea
⇨ decorate a Christmas tree

Grammar Focus 1

● **Prepositions of Time : in & on**

- We use prepositions of time to talk about when something happens. We use *on* for days of the week, dates, celebrations and holidays with the word day in them. We use *in* for parts of the day and with months, seasons and years.

on		in
on Saturday(s), Saturday night on Christmas Day on Friday morning on Wednesday on May 25, 2012, June 6	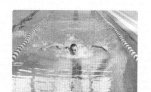 Q: When do you go swimming? A: I go swimming on Saturdays / in the summer.	in the morning, evening in April, May, June in (the) summer, winter in 1999, 2002

Grammar Focus 2

● **Infinitive of Purpose**

- We use an infinitive to explain the purpose of an action. It often answers the questions why? In more formal English, we use *in order to* to explain a purpose.

Q: Why did Cathy go to the library?

A: She went to the library to find some books.
   She went to the library in order to find some books. (Formal)

A. Fill in the blanks with *on* or *in* and match the questions to the correct answers.

1. When do they go to church?   •

2. When is the concert?   •

3. When does the speech contest take place?   •

4. When does she go shopping?   •

• a. She goes shopping _____ Saturdays.

• b. They go to church _____ Sundays.

• c. The concert is _____ November 20th.

• d. The speech contest is _____ December.

B. Look at the pictures and match the words to the correct infinitives.

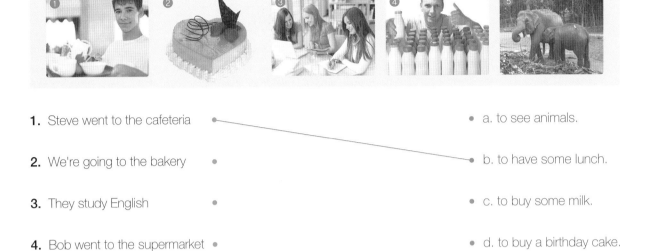

1. Steve went to the cafeteria •   • a. to see animals.

2. We're going to the bakery •   • b. to have some lunch.

3. They study English •   • c. to buy some milk.

4. Bob went to the supermarket •   • d. to buy a birthday cake.

5. We went to the zoo •   • e. to get a better job.

Super Speaking

● Look at the example and practice with a partner. Use the words below or invent your own. (Then change roles and practice again.)

You turned on the TV. Why?

I turned on the TV to listen to the news.

turned on the TV
⇨ listen to the news

called Kevin
⇨ invite him to my party

went to Paris / yesterday
⇨ see the Eiffel Tower

went to Beijing
⇨ study Chinese

crossed your middle and index fingers
⇨ wish good luck

called the hotel desk
⇨ ask for an extra pillow

My Dream Job

Building Vocabulary

A. Match the jobs, pictures and what the workers do.

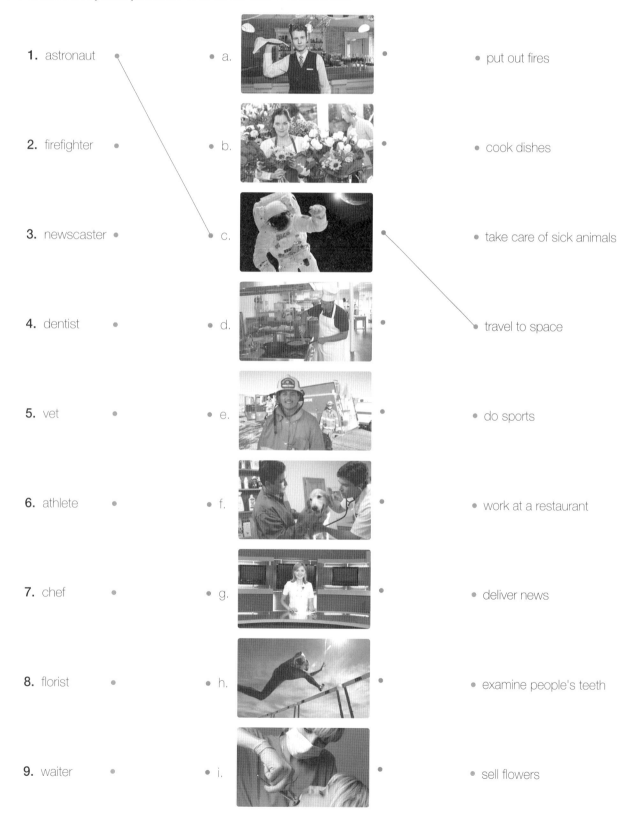

1. astronaut

2. firefighter

3. newscaster

4. dentist

5. vet

6. athlete

7. chef

8. florist

9. waiter

a.

b.

c.

d.

e.

f.

g.

h.

i.

- put out fires

- cook dishes

- take care of sick animals

- travel to space

- do sports

- work at a restaurant

- deliver news

- examine people's teeth

- sell flowers

B. Read the definitions and complete the words.

1. very surprising
   A ☐ ☐ Z ☐ ☐ ☐

2. to decide which thing you want
   C H ☐ ☐ ☐ ☐

3. the area outside the Earth
   ☐ P ☐ ☐ ☐

4. the amount of space between two places
   D ☐ ☐ T ☐ ☐ ☐ ☐

C. Read the below sentences and choose the correct answer.

1. She seems very *polite* and she's very well educated. In this sentence, *polite* means
   (a) behaving or speaking in a nice and respectful way
   (b) behaving in a way which is not polite and upsets other people

2. Are you planning to go *snowboarding* this winter? In this sentence, *snowboarding* means
   (a) a sport or job of catching fish
   (b) a sport in which you stand on a large board and move over snow

3. I have to *babysit* all weekend. In this sentence, *babysit* means
   (a) a small bed with wheels, used for pushing a baby around outdoors
   (b) to care for a child while his or her parents are not at home

A. Complete the three conversations. Choose (a), (b) or (c).

What do you want to be in the future?

(a) Well, I want to be a fashion designer.
(b) I want to eat pizza after school.
(c) What are you good at?

1. What does your older brother do?

(a) I don't think so.

(b) I want to be an actor.

(c) He's a salesperson.

2. Why do you want to be a flight attendant?

(a) I want a job that lets me travel.

(b) I love travel and flying. I want to visit lots of countries every year.

(c) He's going to work in health care.

3. Where are you working now?

(a) Well, I'm trying to find a new office.

(b) Oh, I'm not working yet. I'm still in school.

(c) Many people think this job is easy, but it's usually not very exciting.

B. Read and complete the sentences. Then practice with your partner.

1.

veterinarian

Q: What do you want to be when you grow up?
A: I want to be a veterinarian when I grow up .

2.

journalist

Q: What do you want to be when you grow up?
A: I _____ .

3.

flight attendant

Q: What do you want to be when you grow up?
A: I _____ .

Super Writing 1

A. Draw lines to match the job to the workplace. Then, write sentences as in the example.

1. teacher
2. journalist
3. doctor
4. waitress
5. actress
6. firefighter
7. architect
8. police officer
9. salesperson

- store
- police station
- building site
- school
- hospital
- theater
- TV station
- fire station
- restaurant

1. A teacher works at a school.

2. _____

3. _____

4. _____

5. _____

6. _____

7. _____

8. _____

9. _____

Super Writing 2

- 1~3 Unscramble the words to make sentences.
- 4~7 Sentence Transformation. / N(Negative), Q(Question), T(Tense)

1.

| do | does | what | ? | your mother |

⇨ _____

2.

| there are | in the world | . | amazing jobs | lots of |

⇨ _____

3.

| to meet | would be | every day | . | new people | it | exciting |

⇨ _____

4.

You like teaching children. (Q)

⇨ _____

5.

We discover new facts by using science. (T- Past)

⇨ _____

6.

Olivia wants some cheese on her pasta. (N)

⇨ _____

7.

I talk with my customer. (T - Present Progressive)

⇨ _____

Super Speaking!

A. Listen to the conversation between two people. Then, answer the questions. While you listen, you can take notes. ⊙ Track 95

Listening Notes

	Prepare •••	Speak •••
1. What does she do for a living?	(5 seconds)	(10 seconds)
2. What does the man do for a living?	(5 seconds)	(10 seconds)
3. Does she go to work by subway?	(5 seconds)	(10 seconds)
4. Is he satisfied with his job?	(5 seconds)	(10 seconds)

B. Let's Talk Look at the example and practice with a partner. Use the words below or invent your own. (Then change roles and practice again.)

a pilot
⇨ travel to many countries

What do you want to be in the future?

I want to be a pilot.

Why do you want to be a pilot?

I want to travel to many countries.

a doctor
⇨ help sick people

a movie director
⇨ make famouse movies

a writer
⇨ write many stories about animals

88

S + V-s / Want & Would Like

Grammar Focus 1

● **Spelling Rules in the Third-Person Singular**

- We use the simple present when we talk about what people do all the time, or again and again. In the third person singular (he, she, it), we add -s or -es to the base form.

Every evening, Kevin sits in front of the television, eats his pizza, watches his favorite TV show, and falls asleep.

~ s	work ⇨ works eat ⇨ eats open ⇨ opens write ⇨ writes		• Add -s to most verbs if the subject is singular.
~ es	watch ⇨ watches wash ⇨ washes fix ⇨ fixes go ⇨ goes pass ⇨ passes		• Add -es to verbs that end with -ch, -sh, -x, -o or -ss.
~ ies	study ⇨ studies fly ⇨ flies cry ⇨ cries		• If a verb ends in a consonant+-y, change the y to i and add -es.
Irregular	have ⇨ has		• No rules

Grammar Focus 2

● **Would Like**

- We use *would like* to ask for something. *Would like* is usually more polite than *want*. We can also use *would like* with an infinitive (to + the base verb). In a questions, we use *would* before the subject.

I'm thirsty.
I want a bottle of water.
I would like a bottle of water.
I would like to drink a bottle of water.

A. Write the third person singular of the verb in brackets.

1. Tom (live) _____ in London.

2. She (play) _____ the guitar.

3. He (wear) _____ a suit to work.

4. Kelly (wash) _____ her clothes on Sunday.

B. Make yes/no questions and answers.

1. I'd like a sandwich.

Q: _Would you like a sandwich?_

A: Yes, _I would_ .

2. She'd like a glass of water.

Q: _____

A: No, _____ .

3. I'd like to have a pet.

Q: _____

A: Yes, _____ .

4. Tony'd like to see a movie tonight.

Q: _____

A: No, _____ .

● Look at the example and practice with a partner. Use the words below or invent your own. (Then change roles and practice again.)

Would you like to learn Japanese?

No, I wouldn't. I'd like to learn Korean.

learn / Japanese / ?
No ⇨ Korean

become / a lawyer / ?
No ⇨ a teacher

have / a bicycle / ?
No ⇨ a smartphone

go / to China / ?
No ⇨ to Egypt

Building Vocabulary

A. Look and check the correct words.

1.

surfing _____

cricket _____

2.

volleyball _____

badminton _____

3.

taekwondo _____

yoga _____

4.

snowboarding _____

surfing _____

5.

windsurfing _____

canoeing _____

6.

gymnastics _____

aerobics _____

7.

sky-diving _____

aerobics _____

8.

taekwondo _____

judo _____

B. Circle the correct words and fill in the blanks.

1.

How often do you play _____?

(baseball / soccer)

2.

Which _____ do you think are dangerous?

(sports / animals)

3.

It will be exciting to surf on top of a big wave in the _____.

(mountain / ocean)

C. Match the words and meanings. Draw a line between the word and its meaning.

WORD

MEANING

1.

dangerous

a. problems or difficulties

2.

fun

b. to begin to take part in an activity or game that other people are doing

3.

join

c. likely to harm you

4.

trouble

d. pleasure, enjoyment, entertainment

D. Read the below sentences and choose the correct answer.

1. You must be in great *shape* to run that. In this sentence *shape* means
   (a) the condition or health of something
   (b) to have or use something together with other people

2. She used to work out in the *gym* everyday. In this sentence *gym* means
   (a) someone who does gymnastics as a sport
   (b) a large room where you do exercises or training

3. She is the rising star of Korea's *judo*. In this sentence *judo* means
   (a) a fighting sport in which you try to throw the other person to the ground
   (b) a fighting sport originally from Korea, in which people fight with arms, legs, and feet

A. Read and match. Then practice with your partner.

Hi, My name is William and I'm from Canada. I live in Vancouver. I'm eleven years old. My favorite sport is volleyball. I'm in the school volleyball team, too. My favorite subject is history. Mr. Johnson, the history teacher, is my favorite teacher. My favorite athlete is David Beckham. He's a great soccer player.

1. Who's William's favorite sports star? `C`

2. Where is he from?

3. What's his favorite sport?

4. Is he good at art?

5. Is he in the school volleyball team?

a. Canada.

b. No, he isn't. History is his favorite subject.

c. David Beckham. He thinks David Beckham is a great soccer player.

d. Yes, he is.

e. Volleyball. He's in the school volleyball team, too.

B. Read the texts and name the sports using the words below.

volleyball

table tennis

basketball

soccer

1.
Each team has eleven players. The players have different numbers. Only the goalkeeper can play the ball with the hands.

2.
Each team has six players. The player can hit the ball with the hand. The players are not allowed to touch the net.

3.
Each team has up to five players. The players must try for a goal within 30 seconds of possessing the ball.

4.
The game is played by two or four players. They change their positions. The ball must touch the table on both sides of the net each time it is hit.

Super Writing 1

A. Make conversations as in the example.

1.

> do aerobics   play tennis

A: How often do you work out?

B: Well, I *do aerobics twice a week.*
   And I play tennis every week.

2.

> do yoga   play badminton

A: How often do you work out?

B: _____
   _____

3.

> go in-line skating   play soccer

A: How often do you work out?

B: _____
   _____

B. Read the conversation. Write T for true or F for false. Then correct the false sentences.

> Tom: Do you enjoy any winter sports?
>
> Ava: I'm a huge fan of snowboarding. I go snowboarding almost every weekend. Do you play a lot of sports?
>
> Tom: Yes, I do. I love sports. I play volleyball on Thursdays, and on Saturdays and Sundays I go canoeing with my friends.

1. _____   Tom goes snowboarding almost every weekend.

   _____

2. _____   On Thursdays, Tom goes canoeing with his friends.

   _____

3. _____   Ava goes snowboarding three times a week.

   _____

● 1~3 Unscramble the words to make sentences.
● 4~7 Sentence Transformation. / S(Statement), N(Negative), Q(Question), T(Tense)

1.

| in New York | I | at the Hudson School | . | student | a | am |

⇨ _____

2.

| with my friends | . | I | at school | basketball | play |

⇨ _____

3.

| on the weekend | do | what | do | you | ? |

⇨ _____

4.

Do you work out at a gym? (T - Past)

⇨ _____

5.

I don't know how to surf. (Q)

⇨ _____

6.

We don't have to go to school. (T - Past)

⇨ _____

7.

You need to change your life pattern right now. (N)

⇨ _____

Super Speaking!

A. Listen to the conversation between two students. Then, answer the questions. While you listen, you can take notes. ⊙ Track 104

Listening Notes

	Prepare ●●●	Speak ●●●
1. How often does the boy exercise?	(5 seconds)	(10 seconds)
2. Does the girl play sports on the weekend?	(5 seconds)	(10 seconds)
3. What does she usually do on the weekend?	(5 seconds)	(10 seconds)

B. [Let's Talk] Look at the example and practice with a partner. Use the words below or invent your own. (Then change roles and practice again.)

sometimes / go jogging
⇨ go swimming / three times

How often do you exercise?

I sometimes go jogging near my house. How about you?

I go swimming three times a week.

often / play tennis
⇨ go in-line skating / two times

usually / play badminton
⇨ go weight training / once

sometimes / go bicycling
⇨ go rock climbing / four times

Language Focus! How Often / Can

Grammar Focus 1

● **How Often**

- We use *how often* to ask people how many times they do an activity.

Q: How often does she go to the library?

A: (She goes to the library) Two times a week.

Grammar Focus 2

● **Can: ability**

- We use *can* or *can't* to talk about someone's ability in the present. To make yes/no question, we put the helping verb *can* before the subject.

Alice can play the guitar, but she can't play the drums.

Q: Can you see without glasses?

A: No, I can't.

A. Look and complete the questions.

1. _How often do_ _____ they go to the park?

2. _____ she go to the movie theater?

3. _____ he go on vacation?

4. _____ you go to the mall?

5. _____ Susan go to Paris?

6. _____ the children eat vegetables?

B. Look at the pictures. Then write sentences about what Lisa *can* or *can't* do.

Hi! I'm Lisa.
I'm an elementary school student.

play volleyball (X)   eat with chopsticks (O)

ride a horse (X)   speak Korean (O)

1. *She can't play volleyball.*

2. _____

3. _____

4. _____

Super Speaking

● Jamie is at home with a broken leg. What can he do? What can't he do? Look at the example and practice with a partner. (Then change roles and practice again.)

No, she can't, but she can study at home.

Can Jamie go to school?

go to school / study at home   wash her hands / wash her feet

play basketball / play computer games   play the drums / play the guitar

dance / sing

98

Answers

Unit 01

Building Vocabulary

A. 2. country   3. People   4. shake hands
   5. famous   6. Geography   7. volleyball   8. science

B. 1. c, carry things for people at a hotel
   2. d, paint something as a job
   3. a, serve food in a restaurant
   4. e, sing on a stage
   5. b, make pictures using a camera

C. 1. students   2. to meet   3. class   4. Where

Super Exercise

A. 2. (She's from) Italy.   3. English and history
   4. Britney Spears

B. 2. f   3. e   4. a   5. b   6. d

Super Writing 1

A. 1. name, My name is Sarah Lee. Everyone has a name.
   2. from, Are you from the United States? - Yes, I am.
   3. teacher, Who is your favorite teacher?
   4. live, I live in Seoul. I'm eleven years old.

B. 2. I'm good at gymnastics, too.
   3. I'm good at geography, too.
   4. I'm good at biology, too.

Super Writing 2

1. Our pets have names.   2. In some Asian cultures, people bow in greeting.   3. People greet each other with a hug and a kiss.   4. They may not shake hands.   5. Is Steve from Italy?   6. Is she in the school volleyball team?

Super Speaking!

A. (b) call, (a) meet, (b) What, (a) subject, (b) is, (a) Let's

B. 1. Italy   2. His favorite subject   3. she isn't, in the school volleyball team   4. they aren't, Suji and Steven

Language Focus!

A. 2. are not, are   3. is not, is   4. am not, am   5. are not, are   6. is not, is

B. 2. Is, she isn't   3. Are, I am   4. Is, it isn't

Unit 02

Building Vocabulary

A. 2. left-handed   3. family   4. straight black hair
   5. photographer   6. nurses   7. grandmother
   8. swimming

B. 2. Mark and Sofia   3. Carl   4. grandfather, Mark
   5. older sister, Sarah   6. father, Jason
   7. mother, Sabrina

Super Exercise

A. 2. Victoria Adams   3. Brooklyn   4. Romeo

B. 1. He is David Beckham.   2. He's from London, England.   3. A soccer player.   4. Yes, he is.

C. 2. e   3. a   4. f   5. b   6. d

Super Writing 1

A. 1. my, This is my family. These are my parents.   2. any, Do you have any brothers or sisters?   3. straight black, My mother has straight black hair and has black eyes.

B. eats out - at a family restaurant, watches DVDs - at home, goes shopping - at a department store
   2. On the weekend, my family often eats out at a family restaurant.   3. On the weekend, my family often watches DVDs at home.   4. On the weekend, my family often goes shopping at a department store.

Super Writing 2

1. Scott is left-handed like his father.   2. You look just like your mother.   3. You both have a beautiful smile.   4. Your brother doesn't look like your grandfather.   5. Does your mother have blond straight hair?   6. Are you close to your brother or sister?, I am

Super Speaking!

A. (a) look, both, (b) left-handed, salesman,
   (b) what, wildlife,(a) interesting, eyes

Language Focus!

A. 2. Ann's house   3. Olivia's book   4. the children's money   5. the man's hat

B. 2. her scarf   3. their car   4.our hats   5. his bicycle

Building Vocabulary

A. 1. packing   2. go on a trip   3. airplane   4. fantastic beaches   5. tourists   6. sunbathing   7. scuba diving   8. island

B. 1. relax   2. rent   3. book   4. honeymoon

C. 1. restroom   2. baggage   3. bridge   4. scary

Super Exercise

C. 2. a   3. b   4. d

Super Writing 1

A. 1. comfortable, My hotel is very nice and comfortable.
2. Seoul, Seoul is a big city with a lot of new buildings.
3. any, Did you meet any new people there?
4. population, Its population is about 180 million and the official language is Portuguese.

B. 1. Rome   2. London, you go to London, you will see London Bridge, Big Ben   3. Paris, you go to Paris, you will see the Eiffel Tower, the Louvre Museum   4. New York, you go to New York, you will see the Statue of Liberty, the Empire State Building

Super Writing 2

1. The Amazon is one of the longest rivers in the world.
2. Patong beach is the most popular beach among tourists.   3. The food is delicious and cheap.   4. Have you been to Korea?   5. We're not going to go to Switzerland in December.   6. Are they going to travel by train?   7. We're not going to arrive in Seoul on Saturday afternoon.

Super Speaking!

A. (b) help, (a) absolutely, (b) couldn't, (b) to choose

Language Focus!

A. 2. I'm not going to go to the museum.   3. I'm not going to go to Singapore.   4. I'm going to study English.

B. 1. Yes, he is.   2. No, he isn't. He's going to study English.   3. No, he isn't. He's going to go skiing.

Building Vocabulary

A. 1. yoga   2. rope   3. the Internet   4. a musical instrument   5. to music   6. a skateboard   7. fishing   8. the guitar

B. 1. c   2. a   3. d   4. b

C. 1. fan   2. cycling   3. professional   4. rock climbing

Super Exercise

A. Going out - going out with friends, visiting friends or family, shopping, swimming
Staying at home - listening to music/the radio playing computer games, watching TV/a DVD, surfing the Internet

C. 2. Ben usually studies for the tests on Saturday.
3. Susan often cooks for her grandmother on the weekend.   4. Tom and Jane sometimes play football with their cousins.   5. Caroline is never bored with classes.

Super Writing 1

A. 2. I usually play tennis at the tennis court.   3. I usually go hiking in the forest.   4. I usually volunteer at the nursing home.

B. 2. go to the movies once a month   3. does yoga three times a week   4. enjoy cycling every day

Super Writing 2

1. I usually enjoy reading comic books in my free time.
2. When I have some free time, I like listening to music.
3. I go to watch international games with my dad.
4. I don't play basketball with my older brother.
5. Does she play the guitar?
6. Do he and she spend their free time differently?
7. She doesn't go shopping once a week.

Super Speaking!

A. (a) What, usually, (b) How often, basketball, (a) doesn't, learn, (a) to teach

B. 2. on Saturday afternoon   3. usually play the guitar
4. he doesn't, how to play the guitar someday

Language Focus!

A. 2. I usually have breakfast at 7:30.   3. I sometimes arrive late.   4. She is usually in her office.

B. 1. Yes, he does.   2. Does Ann teach French? - Yes, she does.   3. Do Bob and Kevin play baseball? - No, they don't.

C. 2. What does she have   3. What does he want
4. What do they have

Unit 05

Building Vocabulary
A. 1. orange juice   2. apple   3. hamburger   4. meat
    5. vegetables   6. green tea
B. 1. cafeteria   2. chocolate cake   3. Sandwiches
C. 1. d   2. c   3. a   4. b

Super Exercise
A. 2. Yes, they are.   3. No, they aren't.   4. Yes, they are.
    5. Yes, they are.
C. 2. Yes, I will have a burger.
    3. What kind of burger would you like?
    4. I would like the bacon cheeseburger.

Super Writing 1
A. 2. My favorite food is sushi. Sushi is a Japanese dish.
    3. My favorite food is crepe. Crepe is a French dish.
    4. My favorite food is kimchi. Kimchi is a Korean traditional dish.   5. My favorite food is bulgogi. Bulgogi is a Korean dish.   6. My favorite food is taco. Taco is a Mexican dish.   7. My favorite food is a hamburger. A hamburger is an American dish.

Super Writing 2
1. I have breakfast at seven-thirty.   2. Sandwiches and doughnuts are popular all over the world.   3. Mexican tacos are a Mexican traditional dish.   4. How often do you eat at fast-food restaurant?   5. Are apples, watermelons and grapes healthy?   6. People don't eat fruit in various ways.

Super Speaking!
A. ready, (b) Can, order, (a) like, kind, recommend,
    (b) Both, anything

Language Focus!
A. 1. an   2. some   3. some   4. some   5. a   6. an
B. 3. there is some milk.   4. there is some butter.
    5. there are some vegetables.
    6. there are some tomatoes.   7. there is some meat.
C. 1. an, some   2. some, a

Unit 06

Building Vocabulary
A. 1. dress   2. boots   3. sun hat   4. blouse
    5. short-sleeved shirt   6. a pair of socks
B. 1. shopping   2. size   3. wear   4. medium
C. 2. a hairdresser's   3. a bakery   4. a gift shop
    5. a post office   6. a pharmacy   7. a clothes shop
    8. a butcher's
D. 1. change   2. leather   3. customer

Super Exercise
A. 2. S   3. C   4. C   5. C   6. S
B. 4 - 3 - 2 - 5 - 7 - 6
C. 2. a   3. b   4. e   5. c

Super Writing 1
A. 2. A: How much is this T-shirt? B: It's five dollars including tax.   3. A: How much is this sun hat? B: It's nine dollars including tax.   4. A: How much is this blouse? B: It's twelve dollars including tax.   5. A: How much is this sweater? B: It's fifteen dollars including tax.
B. 1. in the bookstore   2. by credit card   3. window shopping

Super Writing 2
1. I'm looking for a dress.   2. I would like a leather jacket.
3. It looks really good on every lady.   4. Are customers talking to salespeople in a store?   5. What is the price?
6. The students aren't waiting for a bus.   7. Do you like going shopping in other countries?

Super Speaking!
A. (b) anything, black, (a) don't, a little small, large,
    (b) much, change
B. 1. a leather jacket   2. a little small   3. Large   4. $99
    5. I'll take it   6. change

Language Focus!
A. 2. They are painting the house.   3. Nancy is wearing black shoes.   4. He is doing his homework.
B. 2. one   3. ones   4. ones

Building Vocabulary

A. 1. homework 2. breakfast 3. gets up 4. washes the dishes 5. takes a shower 6. plane 7. yoga 8. feeds

B. 2. O, laundry 3. J, snack 4. R, leave 5. N, T, airport

C. 1. watching TV 2. doing the house work 3. playing the violin 4. study in the library 5. read a book 6. ride the horse

Super Exercise

A. 2. has breakfast at seven thirty 3. goes to school at eight o'clock 4. eats lunch at twelve fifteen 5. finishes school at three o'clock 6. does her homework at eight o'clock

B. 2. a 3. e 4. c 5. d

Super Writing 1

B. 2. Jane isn't reading a newspaper. She is sleeping on the sofa. 3. Bob isn't talking on the phone. He is jogging in the park.

Super Writing 2

1. She gets up at 6:30 every morning. 2. I always go to bed at nine thirty. 3. We do our homework in the afternoon. 4. Is the man reading a book? 5. Is she waiting at the airport? 6. They aren't having lunch at the cafeteria. 7. She isn't listening to K-pop music.

Super Speaking!

A. (a) homework, program, go to bed, (b) until, (b) thirty, haven't got

B. the stadium - watching a game / the Internet cafe - surfing the Web / home - watching the documentary program

Language Focus!

A. 2. Is Nancy sleeping in the bed?
  3. Are they walking to school?

B. 2. When/What time do they get to school?
  3. When/What time does Steve leave for school?
  4. When/What time does the movie start?
  5. When/What time do you usually go to bed?
  6. When/What time does the bus arrive?

Building Vocabulary

A. 1. stomachache 2. meal 3. overweight 4. headache 5. medicine 6. exercise 7. toothache 8. bone

B. 2. Y, J, fever 3. J, dentist 4. C, affect 5. B, D, package

C. 1. have a digital camera 2. take some medicine 3. go hiking 4. worry about my weight

Super Exercise

A. 1. go to the dentist 2. get some sleep 3. take it easy

B. 2. He shouldn't come home late. 3. He should do his homework. 4. He should listen to his parents. 5. He should listen in class. 6. He should clean his room. 7. He shouldn't ask for money from his parents every day. 8. He should be nice to his brother and sister. 9. He should help with the housework.

Super Writing 1

A. 2. F, Peter took some medicine. 3. T 4. F, Bob thinks Peter should stay home tonight.

B. 2. He has got a headache. He should take an aspirin. 3. She has got a sore throat. She should have a hot drink.

Super Writing 2

1. Teenagers eat a lot of junk food. 2. Many young people are overweight. 3. I go hiking on the weekends. 4. You shouldn't eat fried food. 5. Did Sarah take a painkiller? 6. Has Lisa got a black cat? 7. Sarah couldn't go to the library because of an earache.

Super Speaking!

A. (b) were, couldn't, (b) toothache, decayed, (b) hurt, (a) feel, fine

Language Focus!

A. 2. have got 3. has got 4. has got

B. 2. shouldn't 3. should, should 4. shouldn't 5. shouldn't 6. should

Unit 09

Building Vocabulary

A. 1. art   2. science   3. English   4. geography
5. physical education   6. music

B. 1. starts   2. After   3. tired

C. 1. c   2. f   3. a   4. b   5. d   6. e

Super Exercise

A. 1. What's your favorite subject?   2. My favorite subject is English.   3. Why do you like English?   4. Because I like my English teacher.   5. Are you interested in math, too?   6. Yes, I am.

B. 1. English   2. physical education(P.E.)   3. geography
4. history   5. math(mathematics)

Super Writing 1

B. 2. Are you interested in history? / I like math.   3. Are you interested in geography? / I like music.

Super Writing 2

1. The school starts at 9 a.m.   2. I have lunch with my friends in the cafeteria.   3. I don't have to get up early because I don't have classes.   4. Does he have to clean up after class?   5. They mustn't bring their cell phones to school.   6. Did you get a good grade in the test?   7. Do they go to different rooms for different classes?

Super Speaking!

A. 1. Yes, they have to[must] wear school uniforms.
2. Yes, he can. But he can't use his phone in class.
3. They have to clean up after class (every day).

Language Focus!

A. 2. You can take a picture with my digital camera.
3. You can use my calculator for a minute.

B. 2. You mustn't speak in class.   3. You must exercise for your health.   4. You mustn't use your mobile in class.

Unit 10

Building Vocabulary

A. 1. birthday   2. party   3. custom   4. pray   5. pick up
6. stethoscope   7. foreigners   8. Thanksgiving

B. 1. parents   2. yarn   3. August   4. general

5. Halloween   6. scary

C. 1. c   2. d   3. a   4. b

Super Exercise

A. 1. (b)   2. (c)   3. (a)

B. 1일 - Independence Movement / 4, 5일 - class play / 21일 - class trip / 30일 - soccer game

Super Writing 1

A. makes party hats on her birthday. She has a big party. She plays the guitar and gets birthday presents.

Super Writing 2

1. What do you usually do on your birthday?   2. Doljanchi is a Korean traditional custom.   3. Parents put various items on a special table.   4. Do they want her to be a scholar?   5. My birthday isn't on November 11th.   6. I went to the movies with my family.   7. Does Peter want to go to college to study economics?

Super Speaking!

A. 1. It(Halloween) is on October 31st.   2. They go from door to door to get candy.   3. They wear costumes to receive the real ghosts and monsters.   4. She goes to her grandma's house. (She greets her elders with a full bow. Then, she gets New Year's greeting money.)

Language Focus!

A. 1. b, on   2. c, on   3. d, in   4. a, on

B. 2. d   3. e   4. c   5. a

Unit 11

Building Vocabulary

A. 2. e, put out fires   3. g, deliver news   4. i, examine people's teeth   5. f, take care of sick animals   6. h, do sports   7. d, cook dishes   8. b, sell flowers   9. a, work at a restaurant

B. 1. amazing   2. choose   3. space   4. distance

C. 1. (a)   2. (b)   3. (b)

Super Exercise

A. 1. (c)   2. (b)   3. (b)

B. 2. want to be a journalist when I grow up   3. want to be a flight attendant when I grow up

Super Writing 1

A. 2. TV station, A journalist works at a TV station.

3. hospital, A doctor works at a hospital. 4. restaurant, A waitress works at a restaurant. 5. theater, An actress works at a theater. 6. fire station, A firefighter works at a fire station. 7. building site, An architect works at a building site. 8. police station, A police officer works at a police station. 9. store, A salesperson works at a store.

Super Writing 2

1. What does your mother do? 2. There are lots of amazing jobs in the world. 3. It would be exciting to meet new people every day. 4. Do you like teaching children? 5. We discovered new facts by using science. 6. Olivia doesn't want any cheese on her pasta. 7. I am talking with my customer.

Super Speaking!

A. 1. She is an English teacher. 2. He is a salesperson.

3. No, she doesn't. She goes to work by her car.

4. Yes, he likes to meet many people.

Language Focus!

A. 1. lives 2. plays 3. wears 4. washes

B. 2. Would she like a glass of water? / she wouldn't

3. Would you like to have a pet? / I would 4. Would Tony like to see a movie tonight? / he wouldn't

And I play soccer every week.

B. 1. F, Ava goes snowboarding almost every weekend.

2. F, On Thursdays, Tom plays volleyball. 3. F, Ava goes snowboarding almost every weekend.

Super Writing 2

1. I am a student at the Hudson School in New York.

2. I play basketball at school with my friends. 3. What do you do on the weekend? 4. Did you work out at a gym? 5. Do you know how to surf? 6. We didn't have to go to school. 7. You don't need to change your life pattern right now.

Super Speaking!

1. He exercises every day after work. 2. No, she doesn't. She hates sports. 3. She watches her favorite programs on TV.

Language Focus!

A. 2. How often does 3. How often does 4. How often do 5. How often does 6. How often do

B. 2. She can eat with chopsticks. 3. She can't ride a horse. 4. She can speak Korean.

Unit 12

Building Vocabulary

A. 1. cricket 2. volleyball 3. yoga 4. surfing

5. canoeing 6. gymnastics 7. aerobics

8. taekwondo

B. 1. soccer 2. sports 3. ocean

C. 1. c 2. d 3. b 4. a

D. 1. (a) 2. (b) 3. (a)

Super Exercise

A. 2. a 3. e 4. b 5. d

B. 1. soccer 2. volleyball 3. basketball 4. table tennis

Super Writing 1

A. 2. Well, I do yoga twice a week. And I play badminton every week. 3. Well, I go in-line skating twice a week.